Stacking Cash
A Server's Guide To Making More Money

By
Mark Cass

Copyright 2021 © by Mark W. Cass
All Rights Reserved

Published by #UpYourAverages Publishing | markwcass.com

First Print Edition January *2021*
ISBN:# 978-1-63795-560-4

No part of this publication may be reproduced or distributed in print or electronic formats without permission by the author. Please respect the hard work of the author and do not participate in or encourage the piracy of copyrighted materials.

Written by Mark Cass | Markwcass.com
Edited by Tim Jacobs | Jacobs Writing Consultants Jacobswc.com
Book Cover Design by Tom Messina | TotalConcept.com

What People Are Saying

"I read a Beta copy of this book and have already increased my tips by 20%. This book is legit." – Taylor D. - server

"This book is excellent. It is a must-read for anyone who is in the restaurant industry. Whether you are a new hire or an old Vet. As a GM, I require all Front of House new hires to read this during their training week." – Sean K. restaurant manager

"As a corporate trainer for a national restaurant chain. I cannot recommend the reading of this book any higher. Talk about making more money and offering a higher level of service; this book is an excellent way to improve your skills tableside." – Zach A. corporate trainer

"Love, love, love this book. So simple, yet so profound." – Misty C. – server trainer

"This book is great. Reading it made me feel more, a lot more confident on the floor." – James W. lead server

Dedications

This book is dedicated first and foremost to my Mom. She taught me the finer art of being a server, floor coordination, and how to work a table of guests. She explained to me at an early age that the "Guests were there to spend money, and to have a good time, and it was our job to help them do both of those things."

Second, this book is dedicated to Fernando Valera, for believing in me and giving me an opportunity when I needed one. Thank You.

And to anyone who is currently working as a server, or thinks that they may someday want to.

This book is for you!

Table Of Contents

Not All Restaurants Are Created Equally
- 'Saving Money' vs. 'Spending Money' Type Restaurants

Showing Up
- Feeling Good and Looking Better
- Early vs. On-Time
- Make Friends With The Hosts

Greeting Your Guests
- Smile
- Bond
- Communicate

Suggestive Selling
- The Power of Suggestion
- Drinks | Appetizers | Entrees | Desserts | Promotional Items

Practice Scenarios
- Practice Scenario 1 | Analysis
- Practice scenario 2 | Analysis

Serving the Food
- Tableside Manners
- Engaging With The Guests
- Serving The Food
- Two-Bite Check Back
- Drink Refills

Closing Business
- Ring It In
- Presenting a Paper Check
- Electronic Billing Vs Credit Card Slips
- Counting Change

Leading By Example
- Teamwork
- Side work
- Strategic Shifts

Table Cloggers - *Bonus Chapter*
- How To Not Let Them Cost You Money

Being Weeded - *Bonus Chapter*
- Being Weeded
- One Task At A Time
- Ask For Help
- Communicate
- Coordinate Your Steps
- Consolidate Your Steps

Just For The GM's
- Increasing Your Production Bonuses

About The Author

Other Titles By Mark

Coming Next *(sneak preview)*

Author's Note

I grew up working in restaurants and developed a love for the industry. Different members of my family have owned, operated, or otherwise made a living working in this industry for longer than I can remember. As a consequence, I began working at my grandmother's restaurant "The Snook Inn" in Matlacha, Florida, along with my cousins at an early age.

They worked in the kitchen with my grandma, and I worked out front as a busser and as an occasional bar back for my mom. I remember being "in the weeds" for the first time at 10 years old on a Friday night. I later worked at a great number of restaurants, from fast food to diners, Bar & Grill chain restaurants, steak houses, as well as ultra-fine dining. At each stop, I learned something and have honed my skills.

Coincidently, I have been in sales and marketing as well, for just about as long. As a result, I have had a lot of success every time I worked on a restaurant floor. In my career, I have consistently ranked among the servers with the top sales, and the highest tips earned. As a result of this experience, I decided to write a book and share some of the helpful information that I have learned along the way. May you enjoy it and earn money all along the way.

Mark Cass | Denver, Colorado - 2021

Stacking Cash

Not All Restaurants Are Created Equal

'Saving Money' vs. 'Spending Money' Type Restaurants

Since most restaurant servers live off of tips, it's a good idea to consider what type of restaurant you would like to work at before applying. Not all restaurants are created equal.

When I worked at a local Waffle House, I earned anywhere from five dollars to seven dollars per table. Occasionally, there would be a ten-dollar tip. At the close of an eight-hour shift, waiting on 10-15 tables, I'd be grateful to have earned anywhere from $75 to $100. That's because Waffle House is not a restaurant where people typically go to spend money. It's a destination for those who are looking to save money while feeding a traveling family of four, or an early-morning construction worker grabbing breakfast before the start of his shift. High volume and low-priced tickets will always equal small tips.

Quick meals and high volume keep you busy and the tips flowing but I was putting in the same effort for a $5 tip that would have been required for a $30 or $40 tip at a high-end steakhouse. I made less money as a server in this instance, simply as a result of where I chose to work. So, the first tip for earning more money as a server is to apply at a restaurant that has high volume and high-ticket sales. Someplace that people go to spend their money. A place known to be popular for date night, family dinners, takes reservations, has a liquor bar, and a line out the door.

If you can't get into a high-end restaurant, consider casual dining chains such as Chili's, Applebee's, T.G.I. Fridays, or B.J.s Brewhouse. This atmosphere will do a lot to strengthen your serving skills, floor coordination, and will usually put more money in your pocket in a single shift than working fast food, or some other "greasy spoon" equivalent.

This is where the journey to making more money as a server begins. You want to work at a place where people go with the intent to spend money.

Showing Up

Feeling Good and Looking Better

Much of how your shift is going to go is determined before you even clock in. Some servers come to work wearing last night's apron and a wrinkled shirt. These servers fail to make the best first impression that they can. No one feels good about spending money with a server that looks disheveled and unclean. So, the next tip for making more money as a server is to arrive well-groomed, with a clean and wrinkle-free uniform. You will like how you feel when you look good, and your guests will enjoy their interactions with you much more as well. Care about how you look and your guests will care about how much they tip you. You're a professional. Look like one.

Arriving Early vs. Arriving On Time

The next aspect lies in the time you arrive. Different places will have different rules about clocking in early, and you will have to operate within whatever parameters are set up at your place of employment. However, I generally have found a lot of success in arriving early. Most places will allow you to clock in if you arrive anywhere within thirty minutes to an hour early.

I like to arrive and clock in 30 minutes before my shift on slower days and an hour early on busy nights. In that hour, I could usually pick up two or three tables that I would not have otherwise had, had I not arrived early.

On top of arriving early, I always volunteer or request to stay late and close. That usually allows for two or three more tables at the end of the night as well. Altogether, arriving early and staying late would increase my nightly take home by about 40%.

Another advantage to arriving early, is you increase your chances of getting a favorable section. If the Floor Manager hasn't yet made the floor plan for that shift, I would find him or her and request a section with booths. *Most guests prefer booths and if you have a section with booths, then chances of you making more money that night increase.*

Looking good, showing up early, and requesting a favorable section would increase my nightly tips by at least 40 – 45%. Done night after night, week after week, that adds up to a lot. Certainly, a significant difference from the co-worker who doesn't do those things.

Make Friends With The Host
This may be the most important bit of advice. Learn the name of your host staff. Compliment them, find something you have in common, and bond with them.

Be sure and greet them and let them know you have clocked in.

They are the gatekeepers to everyone's money. **They determine what server gets sat, how often, and when**. If they don't like you, your pocket will bear the brunt of that, but if they do like you, your pocket will benefit from that as well. Every place of employment has someone who rubs you the wrong way, and you'll prefer not to exchange pleasantries with. Do not let that be the host.

Greeting Your Guests

Smile

You want to greet your guests with a smile and enthusiasm as quickly as possible. They are looking for a great experience and your tip starts the moment they are seated. Make them wait a long time before being greeted and your tip drops. Greet them while wearing all your problems on your face, or act as if them being there is an inconvenience to you, your tip drops even more; but greet them in short order, with a smile and cheery countenance, and your tip increases, as they will decide right then and there, based on their first impression whether they like you or not.

Bond

I try to find something to compliment my guests on when I arrive at their table and make a connection with them. I might compliment their watch, as I am a watch collector myself and can appreciate a nice timepiece when I see one. Maybe they have a baby with them, and he or she is particularly cute. People always like to hear compliments about their kids. I share a little parenting story if appropriate and get a laugh, or maybe their hat is really cool, or we share a passion for a sports team. Something. I look for a way to bond and build on a common interest while they are a guest at my table. A little bit of side conversation with your table goes a long way toward making them feel good about having you as their server. *Not every table affords me this opportunity but I look for it.*

Communicate

The best way to keep your guests happy is to communicate with them. If you are backed up and in the weeds, tell them. "Hi, my name is Mark and I will be taking care of you this evening. I'm closing out a couple of other tables, and need about two minutes, but I see you, and I will be right back with some chips and salsa."

Or some bread, drink order, or whatever it is you are going to come back and do. Just inform them, that goes a long way to a higher tip.

No one likes to sit and wonder about why no one has come to greet them. This makes for a much better impression than no communication at all does. If something has gone wrong, or if there is a delay, inform your guest. Let them know you are working to resolve it. They will appreciate that.

Suggestive Selling

The Power of Suggestion

Having an item to suggest is one of the greatest tools in a server's toolbox. Many guests come in and are looking for a great experience along with a great meal. Trying something new, getting a two for one deal, participating in a holiday special, all work together to make them feel special, and glad that they chose your restaurant. The happier they feel about that decision, the bigger tip they will leave.

Drinks

This usually starts with the drink of the day or an appetizer special. Most restaurants have some sort of deal they are promoting. If you are working at one that does not – then make one up. Servers that suggest items make more money than order takers who do not.

I have sold many featured drinks to guests who would not have ordered one otherwise had I not suggested it.

Become familiar with the menu item you are suggesting, tell them about the item, describe the taste, list the ingredients, tell them how other guests have enjoyed it. Tell them a story. Make them want it.

Not every table will be interested, but many more will order your suggestion than won't if you suggest it to every table.

For example, I like to say something like, "Our featured Margarita of the day is a Watermelon Margarita. We start by muddling a fresh piece of watermelon, and then add a shot or two of our premium Tequila, we top it off with our fresh, made from scratch Margarita mix, and serve it to you on the rocks in a beautiful Martini glass, garnished with a big slice of fresh watermelon. It's always one of our top sellers whenever we feature it. People really enjoy it. Would you like to try one before we sell out?"

I promise you that approach sells more Watermelon Margaritas than asking "What can I get you to drink?" Or by simply stating, "Our drink of the day is Watermelon Margarita, would you like one?"

If you employ a technique such as the first example, you will increase your ticket sales and tips by more than just a little bit.

Or, in the case of the guests ordering their own drinks. Maybe they order a Margarita – you could offer the upsell of Patron, by asking if they'd like Patron? The exchange might go like this

Guest: "Can I have a Margarita on the rocks, please?"

Server: "Sure thing, would you like Patron with that?" Or "Absolutely, would you like us to make that with Patron, our special Margarita Tequila?"
Whatever is comfortable for you to voice.
Get familiar with your house drinks, and what their upsells are. Having them on the tip of your tongue and being able to suggest them at a moment's notice will aid you greatly in increasing the overall price of their ticket. Which in turn increases the amount of your tip.

Not everyone drinks – some people will not be interested in alcoholic drinks, but that doesn't mean you can't still suggest a drink.

I have always made it a habit to suggest appropriate kids drinks, as opposed to letting the parent tell me that they will have water or that they do not need anything. Instead, I suggest healthy drinks to the parents

For example, I might say to the parent after taking their drink order "… and may I bring an apple juice or a chocolate milk for the little one?" Once the kids hear the word chocolate, they usually will shake their head in agreement or utter out some type of verbal confirmation. That teams the kid up with me in our mutual quest to get mom and dad to spend more money. In most instances, the parent will go with one of my suggestions. Not every time, but often enough and that raises the price of their ticket – especially if they have a few children.

For the older kids, I suggest a Sprite if they are in the six to twelve age range.
For the older folks, I always suggest coffee when they order dessert (especially if it's chocolate) or maybe as a 'to-go' drink. When they are packing up to leave and the weather is chilly and I am about to bring them their check, I might suggest a Coffee To Go – sometimes they accept, sometimes they don't, but I sell a lot more by suggesting drinks than I ever did by not.

Each day is different as is each table but if you know the menu, and are in tune with your guests you will see an opportunity for suggestions everywhere, and with each one accepted, your tips increase.

Appetizers

Appetizers are another great way to increase the overall price of your guest's ticket. You need to be familiar with them, and how to descriptively describe them but there is a fine art to selling them. Most people do not plan on ordering appetizers. They are luxury add ons. When selling them, timing is critical.

For example, in a restaurant that offers something complementary to snack on such as bread and butter or some type of nacho chips, you never want to bring that to the table before you offer an appetizer because it will result in a no-sale almost every time.

I always made it a practice to sell them something, preferably an appetizer and drinks, then give them something free after they have spent money.

In the event, you work at a restaurant that greets guests with a complimentary item to sell their appetizers, such as a free basket of chips and salsa at Mexican restaurants, *in order to sell you Queso*.
I would always ask what kind?

For example
Guest: "I'd like to order some Queso, please."
Server: "Sure. What kind would you like? We have two: Plain with ground beef, or my personal favorite, The Cowboy Queso. It has steak and bacon in it. *It's delicious.*"
I sold a lot of Cowboy Queso's that way.

Also, I would try to play a little game with myself each night to see how many appetizers I could sell in a row. I was very intentional about offering and upselling them.

Therefore, I consistently remained in the top percentile of not only the top overall gross sales at any restaurant, but in the top percentile of servers for categorical sales as well, such as apps, drinks, desserts, and coffee.

Entrees

Keep in mind when taking their order, this is a prime time to suggest a premium meal. The more familiar you are with the menu, then the more opportunities you will have to make suggestions here as well.

I always pick the second most expensive item on the menu to suggest This way the upsell wasn't as obvious. Familiarize yourself with the entrée and describe it in the most delicious way possible to the guests.

In general, I approached almost every table with the idea in mind to sell them what I wanted them to have off the menu, instead of them telling me what they want.

Of course, not every suggestion was heeded, nor did every attempt to upsell go my way, but much more did than didn't and I made a lot more money than if I hadn't and you will too. Practice one new upsell each week and within a month you will begin to develop a nice little repertoire of methods to help increase your sales. The amount of money you take home will begin to increase.

The results in your pocket will become measurable. There will be more of it, and it will last longer and go further.

Dessert

I had a suggestion for every phase of the meal including dessert. It's hard to sell both appetizers and desserts – especially in a restaurant that provides anything complimentary but it's not impossible.

You can always suggest a popular dessert when you know your guests are celebrating a birthday, anniversary, or a special occasion. Suggesting a couple take home a dessert to share later is sometimes a worthwhile gesture and a way to overcome what would have otherwise been a no sale.

I often suggest that a certain dessert would taste great later on when they are snuggled up on the couch watching Netflix together. They laugh and nod because they can relate. Sometimes they even take me up on my suggestion, but even if they don't, I connected with them. And this is all right before they calculate how much they want to tip me.

Learn to do that, and your tips increase significantly. It's both an art form and a science. A craft that takes honing but if you become intentional about selling desserts you will be on your workplace's leaderboard soon.

Gift Cards and Promotional Items

Gift cards, t-shirts, baseball caps, coffee mugs, you name it are sometimes offered at different establishments. These are worth mentioning if there happens to be a particular promotion going on, or if your guests are celebrating a significant milestone. They may want a keepsake. A holiday gift card promotion is always an excellent suggestion around Christmas time, especially when the purchaser receives a gift card as well (Buy a $50 gift card, get a $10 card back).

A gift card sale like that is not only great at creating a high percentage of returning customers but it also adds a nice little bump to your overall ticket cost, meaning the addition of special merchandise or a gift card to your guest's check equates to more money made off that table and more money in your pocket.

In conclusion, I will reiterate that the more you hone your suggestive selling skills, the more money you will make.

Practice Scenarios

Server: "Our fresh Margarita of the day is a mixed berry Margarita with fresh blackberries and raspberries muddled together and shaken with our house tequila and our special made from scratch, margarita mix. Can I interest you in one of those this evening?"

Guest: "No, thank you. I will just have a water with lemon."

Server: "No problem. Would you like that lemon with our bottled water or with tap water?"

Guest: "From the tap is fine, and an order of Queso please."

Server: "Sure. Would you care for any meat in the Queso such as ground beef, or steak and bacon?"

Guest: "The steak and bacon sound good. I will have that."

Server: "Okay. I have water with lemon and a bowl of queso for the table? Is that correct?"

Guests: "Yes."

Server: "Okay, I will be right back with this for you."

Analysis

In this scenario of a suggested drink and appetizer exchange, there were four upsells or suggestions made and offered.

1. Featured Margarita of the day
2. Bottled water as opposed to tap water
3. The addition of meat in the Queso
4. A large Queso by way of offering to bring a bowl (as opposed to a cup)

Staying with the Mexican Restaurant theme, let's try another one.

Guest: "I would like an order of Beef Enchiladas please."

Server: "That plate comes with three. Is that okay?"

Guests: "Yes, that is fine."

Server: "A lot of our guests order those covered in our Queso. Would you like to try that?"

Guest: "Yes please, that sounds great."

Analysis

In this scenario, there were another four upsells suggested but they are not as obvious.

1. By informing the guest that the meal came with three Enchiladas they were more inclined to just nod their heads and agree rather than object. In reality, off of this particular menu, there are three ways to order Beef Enchiladas, as a single side, two on a dinner plate, or three on a dinner plate. By offering three and the guest confirming three, the entrée was just upsold from either of the two lesser versions.
2. Further, by suggesting that all three be topped in Queso, and the guests confirming their desire for the suggested idea, each one of those Beef Enchiladas was just upsold by seventy-nine cents, again totaling an additional $2.37 pre-tax in sales on that entrée.

Serving The Food & Working The Table

Tableside Manners

Here's another comparison of Order-Takers versus Servers and showing how your tableside manners goes a long way in separating the two.

I use to always think of myself as a host or a tour guide for my guests and their experience with us at my place of employment.

It was up to me to ensure they enjoyed themselves as well as their food.

I would personally work on a customer appreciation point scale. I made it my goal to earn at least twenty points of appreciation with each of my guests. One for each percent of the bill that I wanted them to leave for me as a tip.

I tried to create twenty instances where I could make the guest appreciate having me as their server.

It starts with making sure they're seated at a clean table. That would be appreciation point one. **Total 1**.

The second point would come by my greeting them within sixty seconds and by doing so with a big smile, a

personal introduction, and communicate with them about what I am going to do for them next.
For example:

"Hello, folks! Happy Friday, I'm Mark and will be taking care of you. I will be right back with some chips and salsa for you. I just wanted to stop by first and introduce myself to you and let you know I see you, and I will be right with you."

You will find your own sequence of words and complimentary items and change that as needed but the point is – I try to garner appreciation points with each table stop. I equate those to dollars being added to my tip. In my initial greeting, I made them smile. They appreciate me greeting them timely, enthusiastically, and with information about what comes next. That's three appreciation points. **Total 4.**

Staying with the Mexican restaurant theme, upon my return, I would place a container of complimentary chips on the table, and a separate container of salsa in front of every person above the age of a toddler and make sure to mention my actions to the table.

"I brought everyone their own cup of salsa, this way no one has to share, and no one has to worry about anyone double-dipping."

They would all smile and nod their heads in agreement, and say "Thank you." Another gesture appreciated leads to another smile and another appreciation point. **Total 5**.

Upon delivery of the salsa, I've already scored five appreciation points. They now like me. They feel comfortable with me. I've made them smile. After building up my likeability factor and scoring a few appreciation points, I'm in a better position to close my first sale. I suggest a drink, and then an appetizer.

When I return, they see that I have thought ahead and placed kids drinks into cups with lids, to better prevent spills. Another appreciation point. **Total 6.**

I get their order right and score another appreciation point. **Total 7**.

Whether it's water with lemons, lime, or Arnold Palmer unsweet tea, I write down their request and then deliver it accordingly, they appreciate that. Always making mention to serve the ladies at the table first. I may say something like, "Here is your Watermelon Margarita ma'am and for you sir, your Bud Light in a bottle." Another appreciation point scored. **Total 8**

Anytime I would serve bottled beer, I would always bring a chilled glass from the bar to the table, and ask if they'd like a chilled glass with their beer.

Most women say yes, and appreciate the gesture, and about fifty percent of the men accept. The ones that don't accept, still appreciate the thought of you going out of your way for them and if they do accept, I always made sure to pour the first glass for them. Potentially two more appreciation points scored with that gesture alone. **Total 9.**

The next step is to take their order and repeat it back to them. They appreciate my effort to get their order correct and the time I took to repeat it to ensure accuracy. Another appreciation point scored. **Total 10**.

Once their order is in, I make it a priority to ensure it is delivered timely, accurately, and at the correct temperature. If there is a problem, I give it immediate attention and seek out the corrective action right away.

This gesture could increase your appreciation point score or the incident could cost you points depending on the severity of the issue and your ability to communicate with the guest, but an accurate writing down of the order and translation to the kitchen will improve everyone's chances of a successfully delivered order.

The ability to communicate clearly, concisely, and accurately is vital. The more you develop that skill, the more your appreciation points will increase and the more money you will make.

Another thought to keep in mind when serving tables and entertaining guests is that it is improper etiquette to ever reach across the table. Many times as servers, we need to reach across a guest's personal space, plate or place setting to hand a plate, pick up a plate, grab a cup for a water refill, or any number of other things. I try very hard **not** to do this. I always make sure to mention my proactive efforts to the guest as well.

For example:
Server: *(holding water pitcher)* "May I have your glass please ma'am. I don't want to reach across your plate."

Guest: "Oh. Thank you, here you go." *(handing over their glass).*

They are happily surprised to hear you acknowledge that often overlooked courtesy.

That's not something most guests are used to hearing. They note that. They appreciate it.
It counts as a double bonus appreciation point. **Total 12.**

In the event I must reach across the table, I always say to each place-setting that I reach across, "Please excuse my reach." Employing a similar set of table awareness and serving etiquette will add greatly to your overall tip total as well.

Engaging with the guests

As I have mentioned earlier, I try to bond with the guests – but not just the adults, the kids too.

If the parents see you take care of their children, they will in turn take care of you. Bring their drink in a to-go cup, with a lid is often an appreciated gesture that adds to your appreciation point total but so is offering to put a child's order in first with the appetizer, or an offer to bring something specific for a little one such as crackers, a muffin, tortillas, whatever your establishment provides. Think about it, offer it, and your appreciation points continue to tally upward.

If the child is an infant, parents always love to hear a nice compliment about their baby. Try to elicit a laugh or a smile from the little one, I as a parent myself, I appreciate people when they can make my kids laugh. If they're older, ask them about their school, compliment something that they have on. Not always will this method be appropriate for the vibe of the table, but oftentimes it will. Be mindful of opportunities to engage with kids, and the parents will tip you more.

Serving the food

Eating is what they came here to do, so you want to make sure your hands are clean when they see you handling their plates.

You want to make sure to set the food in front of them, again ladies first, children second, and then the gentlemen. Every table won't work that way but many will appreciate your serving order and that will again add to your total appreciation points.

If a plate is hot, inform them of that when you set it down. Also, *never* go over a baby's head with a plate of food. I take pro-active measures to avoid that, and then mention it when I do, so they know I was intentional about my movements.

For example, I might hand the food to someone else to pass down and say, "Can I hand this plate to you? I don't want to carry it over top of the baby."

One time I witnessed a guest go off on a server about passing a plate above a baby's head. I learned from that server's mistake to be sure to never do that, and if I must I verbally apologize *before* doing it.

"I'm sorry, I have no way to avoid passing this over the baby." Parents often do not even think about it. It's kind of like a no harm, no foul type of thing, but they will appreciate the fact that you are thinking about it. Cha-Ching! You just got a triple bonus appreciation point. **Total 15**.

Two-Bite Check Back

Two bites into a meal are usually enough for a guest to decide if they like their meal or not. That's the moment when you should stop at the table and ask if everything is to their liking and if they need anything else. If there is, they will appreciate you being there immediately to meet their need. Another appreciation point earned. **Total 16.**

If there is a need and you aren't there – then you lose appreciation points, and they are much easier to lose than they are to gain. This is important, if they are sitting there without silverware, ketchup, steak sauce, tortillas, whatever else, then it is negatively affecting their ability to enjoy their meal. Let them have two bites, then check back.

Drink Refills

Generally speaking, you should start looking to refill drinks once they hit the halfway mark of the glass. Refill at the halfway point and you earn appreciation points, let the glass sit empty and you lose appreciation points.

When refilling a to-go glass with a lid, I always ask the guests if they will be removing the lid as I do not want to put my hands around where their mouth goes, another appreciated gesture. **Total 17.**

On the last time around, or if they ask for a refill near the end of their meal, I offer them a to-go drink. Whether they accept or decline, I still earned additional appreciation points. **Total 18.**

Closing Business
(And A Chance To Earn Bonus Points)

Ring It In

Sometimes as servers we bring drinks to the table without ringing them in. We get sidetracked grabbing a side of sour cream for our guests, or any one of a hundred other possible things we might bring to the table before ringing it in. Before presenting them with the bill, is the moment to double-check each item on the bill and see if anything is missing.

Each addition to the ticket not only makes the restaurant more money, but it also brings you more money as well. Guests typically leave a percentage of their bill as a tip.

As servers, we shoot for 20%. More than 20% means you did exceptionally well, your guests were exceptionally generous, or both.
However, anywhere between 15 – 20% is acceptable. Less than 15% means you have room for improvement and did not impress them as well as you could have…either that or the people don't have an understanding of how they are supposed to tip, which sometimes happens. Either way, the higher the bill, the higher the tip. So, ring it in!

Presenting the Check

Just because you are bringing the check to the table, doesn't mean you are out of opportunities to earn additional appreciation points. Several more opportunities to leave a positive last impression still exist, if you know where to look.

After presenting the check is a great opportunity to offer a to-go drink if you haven't already. Perhaps you could extend an offer to pack up their leftovers for them, as opposed to handing them a to-go box. **Total 19.**

Even after this, opportunities to garner one or two more appreciation points are still up for grabs. For example, in the case of a credit card submission, and you are now returning with a paper check and a pen for them to sign and tip you on. I always make an effort to view the name on the card and then to thank that person by name upon returning the card.

"Thank you for being our guest today, Mr. Johnson."

This usually creates a slight upturn of the lips, and a "Thank you," which leaves each of you parting with a smile, and the next thing they do is credit you with one more point of appreciation. **Total 20.**

Then they fill in the tip amount or drop cash on the table. How much depends on a few things, but the biggest contributing factor is how many appreciation points you scored with them.

You leave them feeling good, you make more money. They will tip you more, and may even ask for you by name upon a return visit.

A positive last impression is just as important as a positive first impression.

Leave them feeling disappointed, they will surely do the same for you.

Electronic Billing

Some places have gotten a little more high tech and now offer electronic payment options at the table. In these instances, the server has no control of when payment is executed. So, it's wise then to make mention toward the end of the meal that the payment device is there and includes a survey which the manager rates the staff by, and you would appreciate positive ratings or remarks.

If you work the statement in and sound natural instead of forced or rehearsed, this will likely earn you a rating of "Excellent." Keep in mind, it is hard for the guest to psychologically rate you as "Excellent" and then tip you poorly. So that is a little bit of an insider tip for you.

In the event, you have a choice to present the guest with an electronic payment device that will recommend a tip for them, or a traditional credit card slip that requires them to handwrite a tip amount, you have a choice to make.

Seasoned servers understand there is a psychological difference between accepting a tip recommendation and personally handwriting out a tip.

For example, if I am presenting a guest check to a large party and it is a steep bill – I am going to opt for the electronic payment device. That way I know it's preprogrammed to suggest a 20% tip. I don't want to risk them leaving me a $20 on a $500 tab.

However, if it's a two-top, and the bill is $43.00. Twenty percent of that is $8.60, an electronic device will suggest that as a 20% tip and they click "OK" and run their credit card. Congratulations you just made $8.60.

Let's say you brought that table a paper check and they had to write out a tip and give their signature. Do you think in most cases their brain calculates $8.60? No.

Most people tip with whole numbers or drop cash with no change. So if it's a cash tip, that is more likely to be a $10 bill as opposed to a five-dollar bill with three singles. If they are writing it out to be debited from their card, that usually comes in whole numbers too, that $8.60 tip, just become the number $10 on the tip amount line more times than not.

Knowing which tip amount option to present to them is often a strategic dance. Management probably encourages electronic payment device usage as it makes everything in the restaurant run easier, but sometimes you make more money by not presenting that option.

Another example might be what we call "Comps." An electronic payment device is going to recommend a 20% tip based on the amount owed, not the original price of the ticket.

Let's say it's a $100 ticket and the guest has a $50 gift card. After the card is applied, the bill is reduced from $100 to $50. An electronic Payment device is going to recommend a $10 tip and show them a big 20% sign. In their mind, they might think that is righteous but had you brought them a paper ticket, in all likelihood they would not tip $10 unless you lost a lot of appreciation points during their visit.

Making Change

This subject could be a course all of its own. There is much more craft in providing a guest with change than one might initially think. How you respond to a request for change can make or break your tip.

What that request really means is I want to tip you, but not this much. The money you are about to return to them, in most cases, is the same money they are going to leave you.

If you bring them a bunch of ones, they are going to leave you a bunch of ones, but if you give them what you want them to give you back, it becomes a game based on strategy.

If we look at that same $43 tab and they hand you a $50 and ask for change, I am going to bring him a five-dollar bill and two singles. Not any other number of denominations.

The guest isn't leaving me the entire seven dollars, or else they wouldn't have asked for change. So, if I bring all singles, I end up with $3 or $4 but if it's a five and two singles, then chances are I get the five.

Or in the case of a $75 ticket and a $100 bill, it's now 20% of $75 which is $15. So, if I bring the guest two ten-dollar bills and a five, they'll tip me a ten-dollar bill along with the five. However, if I bring the guest a twenty-dollar bill with the five, they'll likely tip me the twenty-dollar bill. See how I worked that transaction in my favor?

There is a strategy to employ at every point of the guest experience. Once you learn to look for the opportunities, the higher tips you will begin to receive, and the more money you will make each night.

Leading By Example

Teamwork

Another important aspect of working and earning money as a server is teamwork. It's important to be a good teammate and co-worker because you will need them from time to time.

Occasionally you are going to have more guest requests than you can handle in a timely fashion and will need to lean on a co-worker to help you out. You will need someone to grab an appetizer for you, run your food, or catch a drink refill.

If you are not the kind of co-worker who helps others, then you will be hard-pressed to find co-workers who are willing to help you.

Poor service can cost you money, just as a great teammate can help you make money; but to have to be a team player. **If you want to make more money in tips, then help your co-workers out - even if you are busy.**

They will also be busy when you ask them, but they will stop and help you if you stop and help them. **Everyone does better together**.

Side work

Co-Workers and teammates will judge you based on how well you handle your own and how much you help them. Managers, however, will make judgments about you based on your overall performance, which also includes side work.

I've never met a server who has been thrilled about having to do side work. However, the better job you do, the more trust and confidence you build with the management staff, and they come to know they can rely on you. Once you receive that status and have earned the right to be trusted and counted on by management the better shifts and sections you will be assigned. Which then opens the door for, you guessed it, earning more money.

Strategic Shifts

Every restaurant has strategic shifts—shifts that are busier than others. Some that are preferable to work as opposed to some that are not. Once you've implemented the practices in this book, earned a reputation as a solid server, and consistently rank among the servers with top sales, who do you think will land the best shifts? You will be in a better position to request the coveted shifts and better shifts equal more money in your pocket.

The less you implement, then the more "less preferable" shifts you will have. In many aspects, how much you make as a server is totally up to you.

Table Cloggers
How To Not Let Them Cost You Money
(Bonus Chapter)

As a server, from time to time, you will encounter what I refer to as 'table cloggers.' Guests who just sit at your table and chit-chat and are oblivious to the fact that they are denying you an opportunity to make money from the next people waiting in line.

In a perfect world, these guests would tip large to help compensate you for the money you lost by their extended conversation – but very often you will not be overly compensated in these circumstances. These guests act as a liability to your section as opposed to an asset to your pocket. Learning to minimize their impact and how to deal with these guests politely, and professionally but in a way that mitigates your losses, is another way to increase your nightly take-home pay.

They may order a meal, or they may just order an appetizer to share. However, they just continue to sit there and clog up your table which costs you money.

An order-taker would get frustrated, act unprofessional, and lose money.

On the other hand, a server is savvy and understands these guests are entitled to enjoy the ambiance of the restaurant and the company of each other just as much as you would be if you were the guest and they were the server. Yet, the longer they sit, the more they hold your money up.

Clear The Table: The first clue you can provide for your guests is to clear their table of all dishes, except water glasses, if they haven't yet paid – or if they have paid, remove their water glasses as well and leave them to sit and chat over an empty table.

Wipe Down The Table: After about three to four minutes, if your talkative guests remain, then you can go over with a clean damp cloth and begin to casually wipe the table down.

Invite Them To Move: If after fifteen or twenty minutes, your guests still remain you could extend an invitation to take their conversation to the bar, after explaining that they have the next guests waiting for that table. This is best presented by the manager but in some instances, could be an appropriate invitation to extend as a server as well.

Never ask them to leave though. They are still your guests, paid their money, and should get to enjoy the ambiance too.

In the Weeds

(Bonus Chapter Two)

Being Weeded

When you are overwhelmed with guest requests and starting to give service that is less than your best, we in the restaurant industry refer to that as being "in the weeds," or "being weeded."

This is a tough time for all servers, as the money you earn is based on the level of customer service you provide, and when you are weeded, then you are certainly not at your best.

It's easy to be a great server and give exceptional service when you only have one table, but when you already have three and the host sits down three more tables, full of new families that are all hungry and ready to eat and drink, how well you handle that will determine if you're a good server or not.

The weak ones quit. The order takers crumble under a bevy of mistakes, but the servers rise to the challenge and rake in the cash.

One Task At A Time

I remember one time working the fry station at a very popular high-volume restaurant. My responsibility was preparing and cooking all the fried food. One night there were 100+ tickets in front of me. I almost freaked out. The servers needed their orders pronto.

For a moment I wasn't sure how I was going to handle all of that. I felt a ball of anxiety rising up within me, then clarity came. "One ticket at a time," I told myself.

I looked up and dropped the order for the ticket that was next, then went to the next ticket, and then the next. Within 45 minutes, I had all those ordered cooked, plated, and out to the tables.

So that is my advice to anyone who feels they are being weeded on the floor—or in life—just take it one ticket at a time, or one table at a time, one task at a time. You can only do your best. No one can ask for more than that.

Ask For Help

Don't be afraid to ask for help. If you have been a good solid teammate, then your co-workers will have your back. You can also ask a floor manager to greet a table, grab a drink from the bar, whatever need be. You are all working as a team.

Communicate

Let your guests know you have been double sat, or that you also have a table way over on the other side of the restaurant, or that it will be just a moment and you will be back. Whatever it is, let them know.

Coordinate Your Steps

Floor coordination is of vital importance. As you become more familiar with your floor's layout, table numbers, and flow of kitchen traffic, the better you will be on your feet.

Consolidate Steps

The more things you can grab for as many tables as possible, the better. If table 25 needs butter and you are bringing an appetizer to table 24, then grab the butter and deliver them both on the same trip.

The better you get at consolidating your steps, the less weeded you will be, and the quicker you will get out of the 'weeds'.

For The GM's

If you are a GM for a restaurant and have made it this far in the book, then I thank you for taking the time to read this and I hope you see the value this book has for your staff.

The increase of sales on the floor, the higher the performance bonuses.

I have spent years in the restaurant industry and have found the best way to encourage server upsells are incentive rewards and internal competitions.

Shift competitions are common, such as who can sell the most apps, featured drinks, or even a "perfect ticket" contest consisting of an appetizer, alcoholic drink, nonalcoholic drink, at least two entrees, dessert, and sometimes, even an after-dinner drink.

I encourage routine shift competitions but also weekly competitions, or monthly competitions with bigger incentives.

I once worked at an establishment that gave away a $50 Wal-Mart gift card to the server who got the most positive comment cards in a week. That kept us grinding out every day, every shift.

How can you incentivize your team? What would you like them to sell more of? How much would you like to increase your gross revenue?

Contact me and I can help you and your sales team get there, by designing a training specifically designed around your menu, that will teach your staff to sell those items as opposed to just taking orders.

I will help your management team create incentivized programs to encourage proactive selling from your server staff.

For more information, please feel free to contact me at markwcass.com.

About The Author

Mark Cass is available to speak, mentor, and train in the areas of sales, motivation, personal development, digital marketing, and entrepreneurship.

He is the founder of the Facebook Group *'Up Your Averages'* and author of *'3 Ways To Reach The Top Of Google – The Quick Way, The Right Way, and The Expensive Way'*, and *'Really Good At Barely Getting By'* along with his memoir series, *'The Pursuit of Freedom'*.

Mark is a South Florida native who splits time between Denver, Colorado, and Southwest Florida. He has numerous years of sales training, restaurant experience, and business management.

As a former Chapter President and Training & Development Coordinator for Master Networks (a professional national networking organization), Mark was the recipient of their 2016 Annual Culture Keeper Award.

Other Titles by Mark

The Pursuit of Freedom is a two-volume memoir series about Mark Cass's life. It includes *The Jungle* which covers Mark's life when he's facing time in prison as an adolescent for a crime he did not commit. He spares no details regarding the horror of what life is like on the inside, but he also somehow manages to remain optimistic through it all as he shares his poetry and details of his personal experiences that he had with God during this time. His transparency is sure to make you laugh, cry, and cheer.

In volume two, *Serial Entrepreneur,* Mark starts out describing the first morning he awoke to freedom (being released) and continues with the challenges of seeking employment as a "Returning Citizen." He describes how these challenges led him to start his own business. From there, he explains how he used that experience to start several more businesses, expanded to Texas, and then goes on to describe what it was like to stand on a national stage and be recognized for his outstanding achievement in the business community. He also touches on the day he met the Governor of Florida and requested a pardon. Mark's writing takes you deep inside your emotions and is sure to serve as an inspiration to every person who reads it.

3 Ways to Reach the Top of Google is a comprehensive guide for entrepreneurs on how to make their business visible on the internet and how to get a higher ranking business listing on Google as well as the other top search engines.

If you're a business owner or marketing manager and you are looking for more exposure on the internet. Or maybe just looking for a better understanding of what it takes to get your business listed, and ranking on the search engines. Then this book is for you.

It goes over the 3 different methods for achieving 'getting your business listed at the top of local search engines.

This book covers basic information and strategies for ranking in the top 3 of local map searches, as well as ranking organically through the content on your website, and of course, there is much to be said for pay-per-click advertising as well. It's all covered here.

You will want to keep this book around for reference for years to come. The information is invaluable.

Coming Next
Sneak Preview

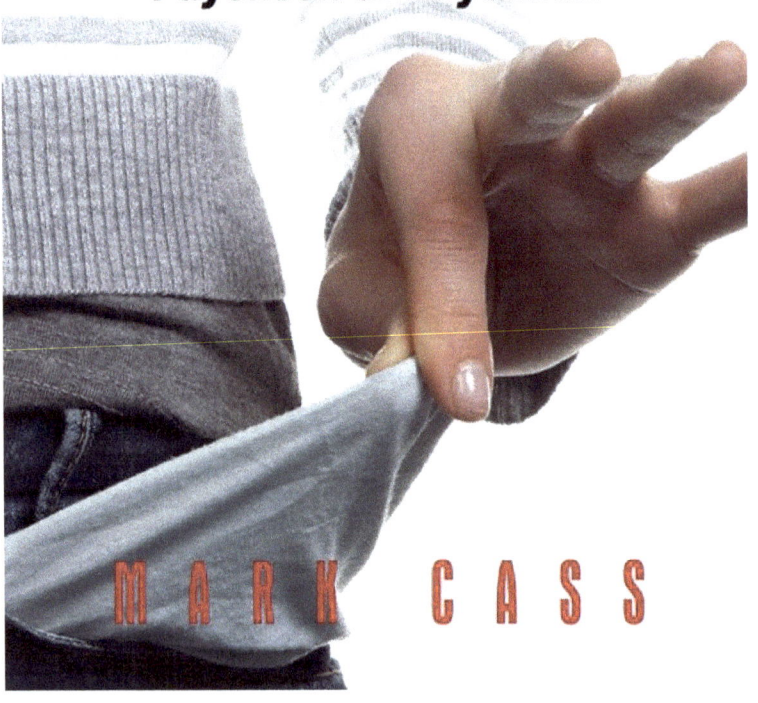

Ever had just enough money to get halfway through the week, but not enough to get through the other half? Ever needed a helping hand till payday, a small loan for gas or groceries, *till Friday?*

How's your credit? Looking to raise your score quickly? Are you open to learning a few tips, tricks, and strategies, on how to significantly raise your credit score quickly?

What about being short on cash to buy a new car, or start a business? Maybe this day finds you looking for creative ways to make money? Ways you hadn't thought of before.

I cover all of that and more within the following pages. Take a look at the table of contents and you will chapters with titles such as

- How to fill up your gas tank for $1.
- Never pay for airport parking again.
- How to buy a car with no money.
- How to significantly raise your credit score quickly.

I can write about these subjects because I lived them. These are methods, ways, and means that I used, learned, and developed when I was 'broke down and doing bad'. I've been there. I've done that. And in this book, I will teach you how to, too. Of all the books I have authored, this one by far is my favorite.